# BRAIN WA

## Designing and Making

## Primary Design

Elaine Baker
Brian Hillary
Chris Hillary
Steve Noon
Patricia Ruff

A SCHOLARSTOWN
*COPYMASTER*

© 1989 Scholarstown Educational Publishers, on behalf of the authors.

**ISBN 1 85276038 9**

First published 1989
by Scholarstown Educational Publishers Ltd.
Albert House, Apex Business Centre, Boscombe Road, Dunstable LU5 4RL

Covers by Terry Bambrook
Illustrations by Elaine Baker
Technical Illustration by Jason Clark

Printed in Great Britain by Kenley Press, Dunstable

Scholarstown
Educational
Publishers

# CONTENTS

# INTRODUCTION

**Brain Waves Designing and Making** aims to help teachers to recognise the potential for designing and making activities within their current classroom practice. Design problems should arise naturally out of pupils' classroom experience and can extend and enrich on-going work. Many curriculum areas provide contexts for design work. It may be that only a slight change of emphasis is required to provide a rich source of starting points for problem-solving activity. Once potential learning situations have been identified it is then a matter of how the task is presented, how the problems are posed and the style of the questions asked.

**Designing and Making** activities offer material relevant to many primary classroom topics :

| TOPIC/THEME | PRIMARY DESIGN SHEETS | TOWARDS TECHNOLOGY SHEETS |
|---|---|---|
| ANIMALS AND BIRDS | 43, 53, 55, 58 | 41, 43, 45, 53 |
| BUILDINGS/STRUCTURES | 11, 56, 57, 58 | 19, 23, 29, 31 |
| CASTLES | 56 | 19, 51 |
| CLOTHES | 39, 41, 45, 53 | |
| COMMUNICATION | 15, 21, 25, 35, 47, 51 | 21, 35, 43, 55, 57 |
| FAMILIES AND HOMES | 11, 23, 55, 56 | 33, 39, 43, 55, 57 |
| FANTASY | 13, 45, 53 | |
| FLIGHT | 43 | 27, 41 |
| FOOD | 25, 41, 43 | 41 |
| LIGHT | | 33, 35 |
| MONEY | 25, 49 | |
| MOVEMENT | 13, 15, 27, 29, 57, 58 | 11 - 25, 39, 45, 47, 49, 53 |
| RECREATION/SPORT | 17, 47, 55, 57 | 11, 13, 15, 35, 37, 47, 49 |
| SAFETY | 19, 33, 37, 41 | Applies to most sheets |
| SENSES/FEELINGS | 27 | 33, 39, 57 |
| SOUND | 19, 21, 23 | |
| TRANSPORT | 55, 57, 58 | 19, 21, 25, 31 |
| WATER | 11 | 19 |
| WEATHER/SEASONS | 43 | 41, 51 |
| WEIGHT | | 15, 23, 27, 51 |

The cross curricular nature of design provides a framework within which pupils can develop a wide range of intellectual, social and physical skills. The design problems provide practical learning experiences which should develop a 'questioning' approach and through which pupils will recognise the need to find out. They should encourage a purposeful use of materials and techniques and develop skills, concepts and attitudes.

| SKILLS | | CONCEPTS | | ATTITUDES |
|---|---|---|---|---|
| observation | measuring | movement | shape | co-operation |
| investigation | cutting | energy | colour | self-discipline |
| analysis | joining/fixing | control | size | independent thinking |
| estimation | modelling | strength | properties of | open-mindedness |
| evaluation | fitting/shaping | structure | materials | originality |
| | assembling | | | flexibility |
| | | | | critical thinking |

# DESIGNING AND MAKING ..... not simply a matter of the finished product?

The process pupils go through when they proceed from problem to solution is the essence of designing and making. Pupils will observe, identify needs, research, plan, make, test, evaluate and modify.
The design process has traditionally been represented by a design 'loop'.

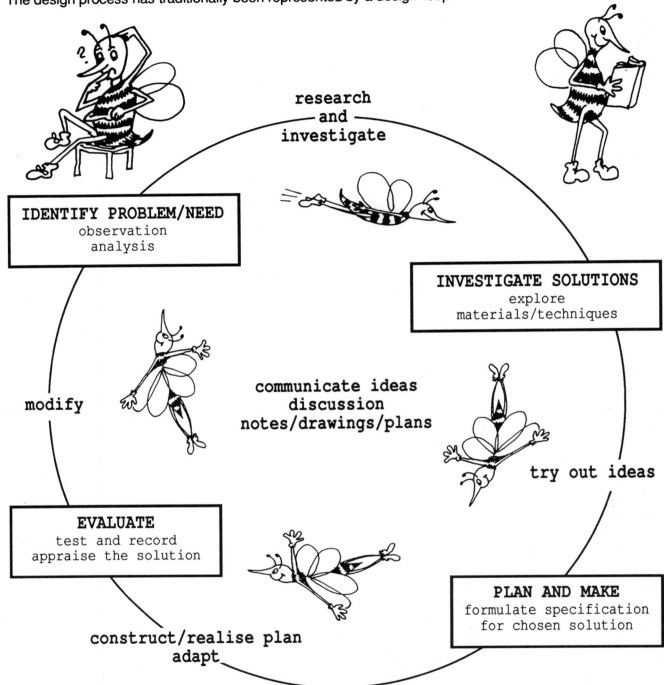

research
and
investigate

**IDENTIFY PROBLEM/NEED**
observation
analysis

**INVESTIGATE SOLUTIONS**
explore
materials/techniques

modify

communicate ideas
discussion
notes/drawings/plans

try out ideas

**EVALUATE**
test and record
appraise the solution

**PLAN AND MAKE**
formulate specification
for chosen solution

construct/realise plan
adapt

It must be recognised however that a step-by-step progression from one stage to the next is not implied. While planning a course of action pupils may identify a need for further research into suitable materials or for investigation of a particular technique. Evaluation and subsequent modification of the plan will then take place.

> 'It is important to recognise that the four ATs for Design and technology do not describe a linear process which requires the activity to begin at AT1. Identification of needs and opportunities may indeed be the starting point, but equally the activity can begin from use of materials, from an artefact which requires modification, from critical appraisal and in many other ways.'

National Curriculum Design and Technology for ages 5 to 16 June 1989

# NATIONAL CURRICULUM : DESIGN AND TECHNOLOGY for ages 5 to 16

The four attainment targets set out by the National Curriculum Working Party correspond to the aspects of the design process outlined.

## Profile Component: Design and Technological Capability

**AT1:** *Identifying needs and opportunities*
Through exploration and investigation of a range of contexts (home; school; recreation; community; business and industry) pupils should be able to identify and state clearly needs and opportunities for design and technological activities.

**AT2:** *Generating a design proposal*
Pupils should be able to produce a realistic, appropriate and achievable design by generating, exploring and developing design and technological ideas and by refining and detailing the design proposal they have chosen.

**AT3:** *Planning and Making*
Working to a plan derived from their previously developed design, pupils should be able to identify, manage and use appropriate resources, including both knowledge and processes, in order to make an artefact, system or environment.

**AT4:** *Appraising*
Pupils should be able to develop, communicate and act constructively upon an appraisal of the processes, outcomes and effects of their own design and technological activity as well as of the outcomes and effects of design and technological activity of others, including those from other times and cultures.

*National Curriculum Design and Technology for ages 5 to 16 June 1989*

## How does each activity contribute to each of the four attainment targets?

The attainment targets should not be considered as a linear process nor should the levels within each target be considered as separate steps. While working on a design activity pupils may reach different levels of achievement within each attainment target. A particular activity may cover Level 2 in AT1, Level 2 in AT2, Level 3 in AT3, Level 2 in AT4. Through careful planning any missing levels can be covered by another activity. An analysis of each activity will help the teacher to plan future work in order to provide opportunities for progression. A definitive analysis of each Designing and Making activity is not appropriate as the teacher will develop the activity according to the needs and experience of pupils (see notes on planning and organisation), but an example is given below:

**ACTIVITY:** Teddy's Shelter

| AT1 | AT2 | AT3 | AT4 |
|---|---|---|---|
| Pupils made observations of building shapes, discussed and explained what they wanted. Pupils made suggestions for changes as they worked. | Pupils drew pictures of the shelter designs and gave reasons for their ideas. Pupils explored the use of different materials. | Pupils used materials safely and effectively to construct the shelter. Pupils were able to explain the techniques they were using and why. | Pupils described what they liked/disliked about their shelters and why. Pupils suggested ways to improve their designs. |

The success of a design activity should not be assessed solely on the quality of the finished solution.
The quality of the learning which has taken place in order to reach that solution is a measure of success.
The final solution should not be assessed in isolation but in terms of the original problem or need:

*"My sign looks a mess!"* (I've failed)

*" Is it easy to change?"*

*"Yes but the words aren't very clear."*

*"How could you make them clearer?"*

*"I could try........................................"* (I've learnt about techniques that work/don't work)

The importance of the correct style of questioning is illustrated here.

## USING BRAIN WAVES DESIGNING AND MAKING

Pupils' pages introduce a design problem. Illustrations do not suggest solutions but reinforce the context for the activity. Questions guide pupils' thinking . Prior to photocopying, teachers may modify the problem or questions (see planning and organisation).  A teachers' page accompanies each activity (see below).

## STARTING POINTS........A good introduction is crucial to the success of the activity.  Exploration of suitable materials or techniques may be the starting point with the specific design brief introduced at a later stage.

### MATERIALS

Materials required for each activity are listed.  The term 'junk' materials refers to the customary collection of boxes, food packets, plastic containers etc. The majority of the activities require the usual range of materials to be found in the busy primary classroom.
By extending or limiting the materials available, the range of design options open to the pupils can be controlled (see notes on planning and organisation)

### THINGS TO THINK ABOUT

Questions designed to prompt pupils' thinking through a task are provided.

The teacher's role in promoting discussion of problems and guiding the direction of investigative work where necessary is vital.
Within a 'questioning' atmosphere pupils will soon begin to ask the right questions themselves.

### PREPARATION/EQUIPMENT/OTHER RESOURCES

An indication of useful stimulus material, equipment for testing and commercial kits is given.
The photocopiable 'skill cards' relevant to the activity are also indicated. These cover the main techniques required. Once photocopied these could be mounted on card and used as pupil reference material.  They are intended to support the teacher and those pupils who require guidance.  However it is often best to allow pupils the freedom to invent their own mechanism.

### MORE THINGS TO THINK ABOUT

Hints for testing and evaluation are also provided where appropriate.

Some questions are designed to extend the activity and to encourage pupils to explore further possibilities.

These questions are provided for teacher guidance but in a form suitable for use by pupils, should it be appropriate.

### SKILLS TO BE DEVELOPED

The skills outlined concentrate on the practical and investigational.  Design activities promote a range of social skills including the ability to co-operate and contribute when working in groups, to accept responsibility and to consider the views of others. These are not outlined for each activity but will become apparent and highly valued. Communication skills, whether verbal, graphical or written, will be developed throughout.

### WHAT HAVE YOU DISCOVERED?

The appraisal of the solution will be encouraged by the correct style of questioning.

How could the design be improved?

Does it answer the problem you set out to solve?

# PLANNING AND ORGANISATION OF DESIGNING AND MAKING ACTIVITIES

Several factors require consideration before embarking upon a design activity. The way a project is organised will depend upon both the pupils' and the teacher's previous experience of the design process. Careful management of the time allocated, the materials, the equipment, the working space and the working groups will allow the teacher to emphasise a particular aspect of the design process or a specific area of learning.

### The design task

A narrow focus will provide support for inexperienced pupils and will help those teachers beginning to gain confidence in this field. A task such as '*Design and make a vehicle that moves across the floor for six metres unaided*' will concentrate pupils' decision-making about a clearly defined problem. A wider focus, by contrast, will open up the decision-making about the parameters of the design task itself e.g. '*Design and make something that moves across a flat surface*'

Teachers may wish to 'customise' the design sheets prior to photocopying in order to match the particular needs of the classroom topic or the particular skills they wish to promote. Simply mask out the text on your first photocopy and insert your own.

### Time

The amount of time devoted to the investigation, planning, making and evaluation aspects of the design process should reflect the importance to be placed on each. Pupils should have sufficient time to explore ideas fully and to be thorough throughout.

### Materials

Restricting the materials available for a task will encourage pupils to explore and gain experience of specific materials and techniques e.g. '*Design and make a tall structure using newspaper*'. A limited range of materials will not reduce the level of thinking required but merely focus the direction of that thinking.

### Equipment

The skills of the pupils must be taken into account. Placing too many demands on pupils in one design task ie.new techniques, new materials and new tools may be counter-productive.

### Working space

An area of the classroom which will support the 'trying out of ideas' aspect of the design process will be required. Pupils may need to construct with card, wood or junk materials and they may wish to experiment with construction kits, if available, to make models. Access to resources and equipment should be arranged with safety in mind. Good working practice can be encouraged by careful organisation of the work area with clear labelling of storage points etc. Opportunities for display of models and design ideas should be offered.
Display should not just occur at the end of a project. Work which is currently under construction or in the eartlystages of design should be on view so that pupils can share experiences and information.

### Working Groups

Small group work will offer pupils opportunities for discussion of ideas and for collaboration on specific tasks. Full class discussion will be apppropriate at the introductory stage or when a particular construction or design problem is to be highlighted.
The development of communication skills should be fostered throughout. Pupils should be encouraged to explain their thinking at every stage both verbally and on paper through design sketches and annotated drawings. The use of the correct terminology should be promoted whenever possible and appropriate.

# DESIGN ANALYSIS..................................thinking about design?

Children often have opportunities to be involved in designing and making activities. But how often are they encouraged to consider the world in which they live? Pupils should be able to:

*Describe to others what they like and dislike about familiar artefacts, systems or environments.* [level 1]
*Make some simple value judgements about familiar artefacts, systems or environments, including those from other times and cultures (for example how well it works, how pleasing is the appearance).* [level 2]
*Comment upon existing artefacts, systems, or environments, and those from other times and cultures, in terms of form and function, including appearance, use of resources.* [level 4]

National Curriculum Design and Technology for ages 5 to 16 June 1989

By analysing man-made features e.g. buildings and consumer products pupils can gain insight into the designer's way of looking at the world and can gain fluency in the 'language' of design. A variety of skills and concepts will be developed as they will be involved in observation, research and evaluation.

By studying man-made products pupils will consider some or all of these factors:

| | |
|---|---|
| **Function** | What does it do? What is its use? How **well** does it do its job? |
| **Form** | What size is it? Is the size important? What shape is it? Is shape important? What is it made of? Why have these materials been used? |
| **Appearance** | Is it attractive? Does it **need** to be attractive to do its job? How important is colour? texture? |
| **Construction** | How has it been made? What techniques and materials have been used? Why? |
| **Performance** | Does it do the job it has been designed to do? How well? |
| **Price** | Is it value for money? How does it compare with other similar products? |

By considering these factors pupils will develop the critical skills of an informed consumer. Consumer decisions are based on a balance of aesthetics, performance and price. A dishcloth, for example would be purchased on the basis of performance - there would be no point in buying a dishcloth which looked attractive but which was not absorbent and hardwearing!

Design analysis activity may involve the pupils in dismantling items to find out how they work and it will often be appropriate to analyse items in use. eg. **graters.** Compare different types when used to grate the same foodstuff e.g. a carrot. Compare the results, the time taken, ease of use, safety in use, ease of cleaning, safety when cleaning, ease of storage. Consider the aesthetic factors. Are these important? Which grater scores highly on all the points considered?

Encourage pupils to discuss the relative merits of man-made items. A **Which?** style report is a useful way of focussing pupils' thinking. **Sheet 9** outlines a typical design analysis activity based on pens. The scope for this type of work will be evident but further suggestions are provided below:

## TEETHING TROUBLES!

This type of activity would be easily incorporated in work on dental health. Invite pupils to bring in a collection of toothpaste containers/dispensers. Pupils could study the packaging design. Which one is the most eye-catching? Which one would stand out on the supermarket shelf? Pupils could classify the different types of containers (tubes, pump dispensers, lids, flip tops etc.) A discussion of the problems pupils have encountered when using toothpaste (squeezing out the last bit! .... tops not being put back on etc.) could follow. A test could be devised to compare different dispensers in use (how much or how little can be dispensed at a time ....... how clean the dispenser stays in use etc.) Ensure that it is a **fair** test. Design work could then involve the creation of packaging for a new brand of toothpaste.

...... GLUE DISPENSERS ....... SANDWICH BOXES ....... PENCIL CASES ...... SCHOOL BAGS ......
........ SUN HATS...... PURSES/WALLETS ....... CARRIER BAGS .......
......... FLOWER VASES ......... SKATE BOARDS ............

# PICK A PEN!

Make a collection of pens
Look at them carefully
What do you notice about them?

Try sorting the pens into groups
e.g. felt pens, ball pens, fountain pens.

Think about different ways to compare them
e.g. How easy is it to hold the pen?   What type of ink is used?
How easy is it to write with?      Does it smudge?
How easy is it to draw with?      Is the pen attractive?
Are some better than others on different types of paper?
Does the pen have a lid or top? Does it stay on?
What do your friends think?
Which is the most popular pen?

Test the pens. Decide on ways to compare them and give each one a star rating.
☆☆☆ = good
☆☆ = fair
☆ = poor

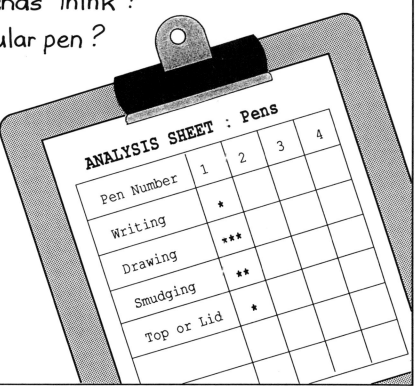

| ANALYSIS SHEET : Pens | | | | |
|---|---|---|---|---|
| Pen Number | 1 | 2 | 3 | 4 |
| Writing | * | | | |
| Drawing | | *** | | |
| Smudging | | ** | | |
| Top or Lid | | * | | |
| | | | | |

# STARTING POINTS.....

An 'observation' walk in the locality to sketch the different shapes and construction of homes and buildings . . . . focus discussion on roof shapes . . . Book research to find out about shelter (through the ages and around the world) . . . Investigation of materials . . . which will keep out the rain? . . . Classification of materials (waterproof/non-waterproof) . . .

## MATERIALS

newspaper (can be rolled to make strong supports)
plastic bags
adhesive tape
string
plastic hoops

(limited materials will 'focus' the design options)

## THINGS TO THINK ABOUT

How can a sheet of newspaper be turned into a strong support?

How can the newspaper supports be joined together to make a strong frame?

How will the roof material be attached to the frame?

## PREPARATION/EQUIPMENT/OTHER RESOURCES

Collection of visual stimulus material - roof shapes, tents etc.

Variety of materials for waterproof testing

Teddy bears!

## MORE THINGS TO THINK ABOUT

How can the designs be tested fairly?

Are they waterproof?

Are they strong enough to stand up to the wind?

## SKILLS TO BE DEVELOPED

**Investigational . . .**

Observation and classification of types of shelter. Testing of materials for waterproof qualities. Exploration of suitable structures

**Practical . . .**

Rolling and fixing supports
Assembly of structure

## WHAT HAVE YOU DISCOVERED?

Which house is the most stable? Why?

Which frame shape is the strongest? Why?

Which house kept Teddy dry for the longest time? Why?

# Teddy Bear

Poor Teddy is feeling very wet. He's been left outside in the rain. He would much rather be inside and dry.

**DESIGN AND MAKE** a house to keep Teddy dry, using only the materials available.

THINK ABOUT— How could you make weak materials stronger?

THINK ABOUT— Will your design stand up to the wind as well?

# STARTING POINTS......

Dragon stories and poems . . . discussion of pictures of dragons from fairy stories . . . research and comparison with Chinese dragons . . . identification of dragon features . . . encourage pencil drawings . . . focus discussion on parts which could move . . . classification of types of movement (up and down/in and out/round and round etc.)

## MATERIALS

card
corrugated card
junk materials e.g. boxes, card
tubes, plastic pots, lollipop sticks.
thin dowelling
wire
paper fasteners
string
materials for decoration (coloured
tissue, sequins, feathers etc.)

## THINGS TO THINK ABOUT

Which part of the dragon will move?
eyes? jaws? wings? tongue? tail?
head?

How will you make the part move?
by pulling a string? by turning a
wheel? with a lever?

## PREPARATION/EQUIPMENT/OTHER RESOURCES

Collection of visual stimulus
material
Stories and poems.
Cutting and measuring equipment.

Skill card nos. 1,2 and 6

## MORE THINGS TO THINK ABOUT

How could the dragon be made to move
along the floor?

How could wheels be attached?

How will you decorate and finish the
dragon? Will it be friendly or
fierce?

## SKILLS TO BE DEVELOPED

**Investigational . . .**

Observation and recording of dragon
features. Hypothesis and testing of
movement mechanisms.

**Practical . . .**

drawing, measuring, marking, cutting,
shaping, forming, construction and
assembly.

## WHAT HAVE YOU DISCOVERED?

Which movement mechanisms were most
successful? Why?

Could you use these ideas for
movement in other situations?

Which design looks most fierce? Why?

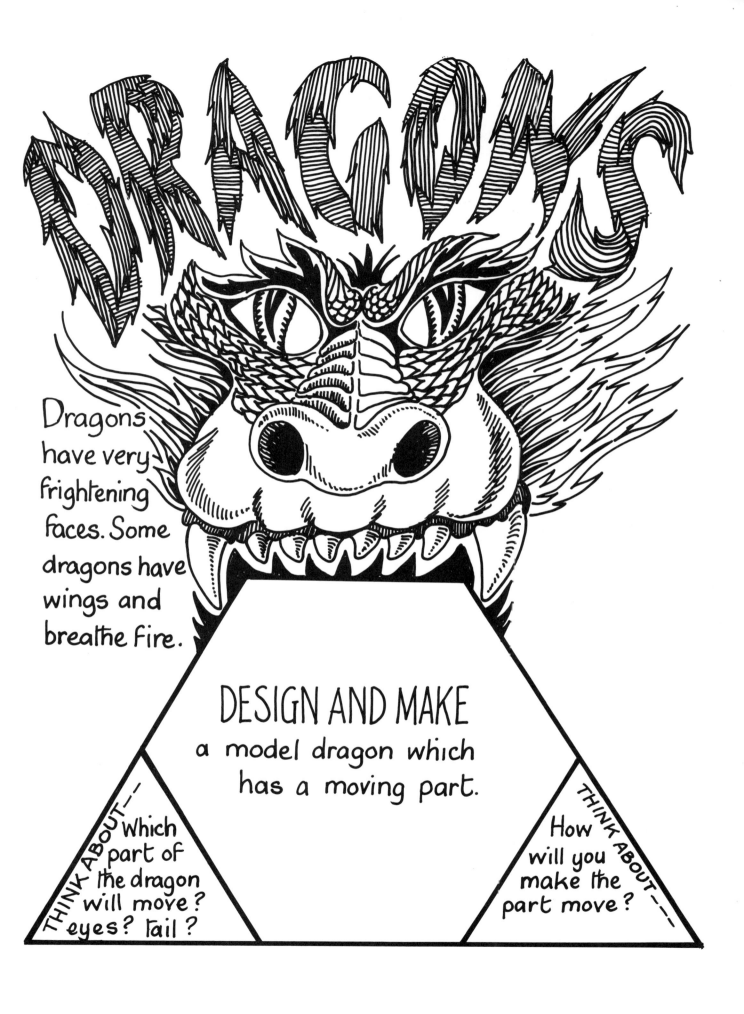

# DRAGONS

Dragons have very frightening faces. Some dragons have wings and breathe fire.

## DESIGN AND MAKE
a model dragon which has a moving part.

THINK ABOUT — Which part of the dragon will move? eyes? tail?

THINK ABOUT — How will you make the part move?

# STARTING POINTS......

A 'brainstorm' session about the sort of books pupils enjoyed when they were younger . . . a display fo young children's books . . . discussion on simplicity of drawings and clarity of text .. . focus on those books with hidden or surprise objects . . . investigation of methods for concealing and revealing parts of the illustration . . .

## MATERIALS

paper
card (various thicknesses)
paper fasteners
string
adhesive
staples

## THINGS TO THINK ABOUT

Where will the objects be hidden?
behind doors?
in cupboards?
under carpets?
under cushions?
in boxes?
in cages?
under leaves?
under stones?

## PREPARATION/EQUIPMENT/OTHER RESOURCES

Local library display of childrens' books on loan.  Visit from librarian/author/illustrator.

Ask pupils to bring in examples from home.

Cutting and measuring equipment.

Skill card nos. 1, 2, 4 and 6

## MORE THINGS TO THINK ABOUT

Are the moving parts suitable for little fingers?

The books will be used again and again.  How could the moving parts be made to last a long time?

Test the books with young children.

## SKILLS TO BE DEVELOPED

**Investigational . . .**

Observation and analysis of mechanisms to hide and reveal. Exploration of suitable techniques

**Practical . . .**

Measuring, marking, cutting, joining and fixing  Drawing with imagination and accuracy.

## WHAT HAVE YOU DISCOVERED?

Which pages of the book were the most successful?

Why were they popular?

Which mechanism was the easist to construct?

Which mechanism was the easiest to use?

This page may be photocopied for classroom use only

# HIDE AND SEEK

**DESIGN AND MAKE** a book for pre-school children with hidden objects to surprise and delight the reader.

THINK ABOUT— How will the objects be hidden and revealed?

THINK ABOUT— Which parts of the story will be hidden?

# STARTING POINTS ...... A survey of board games popular in the class

or school . .. recording of results on a graph..... analysis of results . . .

....links with mathematical concepts (shape, tessellation, number) and language work (writing instructions) . . .

## MATERIALS

2cm squared paper
card board
adhesive tape
coloured crayons/pens
clear adhesive covering
cocktail sticks
paper fasteners
rulers
set squares
clay (for moving pieces)

## THINGS TO THINK ABOUT

How will players move across the board? Throwing dice? Turning a spinner?

Will the game be about chance or will the players need to use their brains?

## PREPARATION/EQUIPMENT/OTHER RESOURCES

Selection of shape templates
counters
dice
safety knives and rulers
collection of commercial board games

Skill card no. 4

## MORE THINGS TO THINK ABOUT

Will your game last a long time?

How could you make it more hardwearing?

Will the game pack away easily? Design a package for it.

Test your game with friends.

## SKILLS TO BE DEVELOPED

**Investigational** . . .

Observation and analysis of existing board game designs.
Testing of ideas.

**Practical** . . .

measuring, marking, cutting

## WHAT HAVE YOU DISCOVERED?

Did your friends enjoy the game?
How long did the game last?

How could you make it more difficult? more exciting? more interesting?

Did your friends understand the rules? Are they clear?

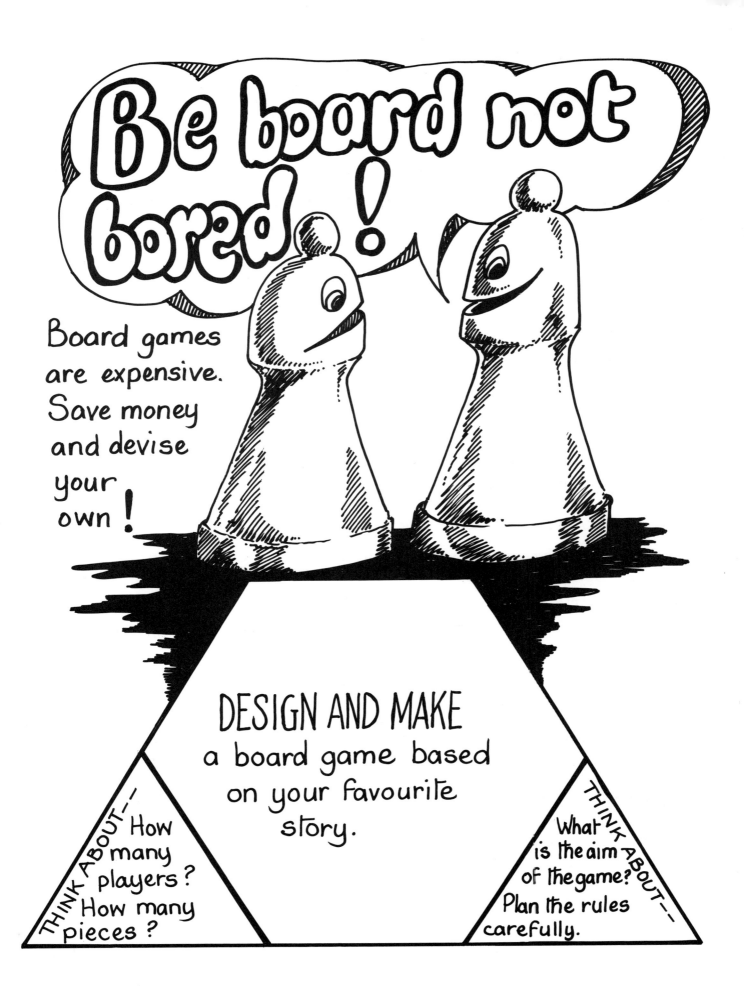

# STARTING POINTS ......

An investigation into ways of producing sound using everyday objects . . . collection of musical instruments to classify according to the way the sound is produced (percussion/wind/string) . . . focus on a design task . . . (design ananylis of existing children's toys with emphasis on safety and suitability for young child ). . .

## MATERIALS

thick card
wood
dowelling
plastic tubing
junk materials eg. cotton reels,
lollipop sticks, sealable tins,
plastic tubes
string
strips of leather/felt
adhesive tape

## THINGS TO THINK ABOUT

Will the design be suitable for a young child?

Think about their age and ability.

Think about size and weight.

Will it be safe for a child?

Think about sharp edges and sharp points.

## PREPARATION/EQUIPMENT/OTHER RESOURCES

A collection of musical instruments.

A collection of childrens toys for safety analysis

Cutting tools for wood, plastic and fabric.

## MORE THINGS TO THINK ABOUT

Have you joined and sealed the toy safely?

Will it break when dropped?

Remember that small parts could be swallowed.

Remember that children suck things. What paint have you used?

## SKILLS TO BE DEVELOPED

**Investigational . . .**

Research into ways of making sound. Hypothesis and testing for safety.

**Practical . . .**

Physical experience of a wide range of materials and properties. Assembly skills

## WHAT HAVE YOU DISCOVERED?

How many different types of sound has your class prdouced?

How could your design be made safer?

What do young children think of your toys?

# STARTING POINTS . . . . . .

Making musical instruments from junk materials (see Shake Rattle and Roll sheet 18) . . . experimentation with everyday objects to produce sound effects . . . discussion of sounds required for a particular story or poem . . . a planning session could involve the concept of a musical score (this could be pictorial) . . .

## MATERIALS

junk materials eg. boxes, pots, card tubes, tins etc.
beads
dried peas and beans
elastic bands
fishing line
wire
string
balloons
adhesive tape

## THINGS TO THINK ABOUT

How can sounds be made?
banging? shaking? rattling?
stretching? blowing?

Can your voice be used to make different sounds?

What sounds will you need?
rain? wind? footsteps? traffic?

## PREPARATION/EQUIPMENT/OTHER RESOURCES

Selection of musical instruments

Bicycle pumps and other everyday objects to make sounds

Recording equipment.

## MORE THINGS TO THINK ABOUT

How can you express different ideas in sound?
happiness? sunshine? sadness? mist and fog?

How will you remember what to play and when? Work out a system

## SKILLS TO BE DEVELOPED

**Investigational** . . .

Practical research into sound making

**Practical** . . .

assembly of musical instruments, recording

## WHAT HAVE YOU DISCOVERED?

Play back your recording.

Are some sounds too loud or too soft?

This page may be photocopied for classroom use only

# Soundtrack

**DESIGN AND MAKE** a recorded soundtrack of sound effects for a favourite poem or story.

THINK ABOUT— Which sounds will be quiet? loud? scary?

THINK ABOUT— Can your voice be used to produce different sounds?

# STARTING POINTS . . . . . . .

A study of children's first books for ideas, paying particular attention to colour and simplicity of design . . . focus on safety (the mobile must be secure!) . . . investigate ways of making sounds (rustling tin foil, wind chimes etc.) . . .

## MATERIALS

wire coat hangers
art straws
dowelling
wire, string, fishing line
adhesive tape
junk materials eg. small containers,
card tubes, bottle tops
card (various thicknesses)
felt
tin foil
clay (to make wind chimes)

## THINGS TO THINK ABOUT

How will you balance the mobile?

Think about the weight of the mobile objects.

What safety factors will you need to consider? (Remember that the mobile will hang above the baby.)

Will colour be important?

## PREPARATION/EQUIPMENT/OTHER RESOURCES

Children's books for design ideas.

Examples of existing mobile designs.

Safety knives and rulers

Skill card no. 5

## MORE THINGS TO THINK ABOUT

Could the mobile make a sound as it moves?

What will make the noise?

Test your designs.

Do they attract a baby's attention?

## SKILLS TO BE DEVELOPED

### Investigational . . .

Research and evaluation of children's books for design ideas. Hypothesis and testing of mobile designs

### Practical . . .

Measuring, marking, cutting, joining and fixing, framework assembly.

## WHAT HAVE YOU DISCOVERED?

Which mobile makes the most attractive display? Why?

Which mobile moves most freely? Why?

Which mobile makes the most attractive sound? How?

How could you improve you design?

# Moving Shapes

New born babies will focus on brightly coloured objects that move.

If this baby had something attractive to look at while lying in its cot it might not cry so much!

ah-ah-ah!
ah-ah-ah!
ah-ah-ah!
ah-ah ah-ah

DESIGN AND MAKE a free moving mobile to hang over a baby's cot and attract its attention.

THINK ABOUT-- How will the mobile move freely?

THINK ABOUT-- How will you balance the different mobile objects?

# STARTING POINTS ...... Shopping role-play activities ......

a brainstorm session about the kind of 'props' which might be required for role-play situations at the shops, the Post Office, the library, the Health Clinic etc . . . .
. . . . . a discussion of open/closed signs pupils have noticed themselves . . . . .
What makes them attractive?  How do they work?

---

## MATERIALS

card
paper
paper fasteners
elastic bands
adhesive
colouring materials
coloured adhesive paper

---

## THINGS TO THINK ABOUT

How will the sign change from 'open' to 'closed'?

Where will the sign be placed?

How will it be fixed in position?

Will it be viewed from both sides?

What shape will the sign be?

---

## PREPARATION/EQUIPMENT/OTHER RESOURCES

Lettering templates/stencils
Shape templates/stencils

Examples of lettering styles

Collection of logos for different shops.
Safety knives and rulers

Skill card nos. 1, 2 and 6

---

## MORE THINGS TO THINK ABOUT

Could the sign give other messages too?

(HINT: Think about what the shop sells.  A fish shape for a fish shop. A medicine bottle for a chemist).

---

## SKILLS TO BE DEVELOPED

### Investigational . . .

Observation and analysis of existing signs
Testing and hypothesis of sign mechanisms

### Practical . . .

measuring, marking, cutting joining and fixing.

---

## WHAT HAVE YOU DISCOVERED?

How effective is the sign from a distance?

How could it be made clearer?

Which sign is the easiest to operate? Why?

---

# OPEN ALL HOURS

Sorry we're closed

## DESIGN AND MAKE

an open and closed sign which can be changed quickly and easily. The sign must indicate the type of shop, and encourage customers to call again.

THINK ABOUT — How will the sign be operated? sliding a handle? pulling a string?

THINK ABOUT — How can you make the sign clear and attractive?

# STARTING POINTS ......

Dance and drama activities . . . . exploration of bodily movements, joints etc. . . . Animation and development of a favourite story . . . . . Religious and moral themes (good/bad) . . . Emotions (happiness/sadness/fear/jealousy etc). The 'focus' of the task may concentrate on movement or character or both.

## MATERIALS

(according to 'focus' of task)
card
paper
paper fasteners
string/wire/fishing line
junk materials e.g. cotton reels,
card tubes, lollipop sticks
scrap fabrics and wool
polystyrene balls
thin dowelling
adhesive.

## THINGS TO THINK ABOUT

Which parts of your body bend?

How can you make a joint for the puppet?

How will you operate the joint?

## PREPARATION/EQUIPEMNT/OTHER RESOURCES

Visit to school by professional puppeteer.

Collection of puppets eg. string, glove, sock and finger puppets.

Reference books on puppet making
A skeleton or skeleton diagram
safely knives and rulers

Skill card no. 6

## MORE THNGS TO THINK ABOUT

What sort of character will your puppet play? happy? sad? angry?

How can you show their character?

Will the puppets speak?

## SKILLS TO BE DEVELOPED

**Investigational** . . .

Observation and analysis of body movements and/or facial expressions. Hypothesis and testing of movement mechanisms

**Practical** . . .

Measuring, marking, cutting, joining and fixing. Operation of puppet.

## WHAT HAVE YOU DISCOVERED?

Which is the easiest way to operate the puppet?

How could you improve your design?

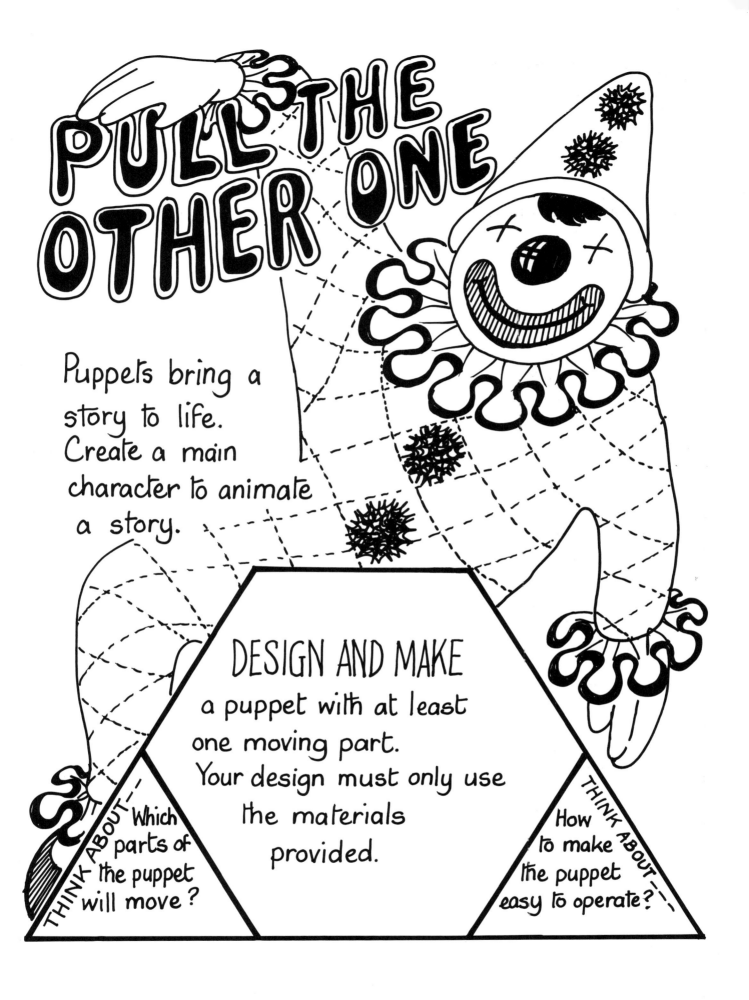

# PULL THE OTHER ONE

Puppets bring a story to life. Create a main character to animate a story.

## DESIGN AND MAKE

a puppet with at least one moving part. Your design must only use the materials provided.

THINK ABOUT— Which parts of the puppet will move?

THINK ABOUT— How to make the puppet easy to operate?

# STARTING POINTS ......

This design problem may arise naturally from puppet making activity or may be introduced simultaneously . . . analysis of space required for puppets and puppeteers . . . discussion of requirements (specific to the type and size of puppets in use) . . . observation of existing 'fold and pack away' items eg. clothes airer, ironing board, display screens etc. to highlight hinge mechanisms.

## MATERIALS

cardboard
grocery boxes, shoes boxes etc.
string
dowelling
adhesive tape
cotton reels
wheels
materials for decoration
wood (according to 'focus' of task)

## THINGS TO THINK ABOUT

How many puppets will be on stage at the same time?

Where will the puppeteers stand? How much space will they need?

How could you use hinges to improve your design?

## PREPARATION/EQUIPMENT/OTHER RESOURCES

Examples of 'fold and pack away' items

Building bricks and constructional apparatus to experiment and test space requirements.

Safety knives and rulers (carpentry equipment)

Skill card no. 6

## MORE THINGS TO THINK ABOUT

Will you need scenery?

How could the scenery be changed easily?

Will you need curtains or a screen?

How will they be operated?

## SKILLS TO BE DEVELOPED

**Investigational . . .**

Observation and analysis of hinge mechanisms.
Analysis of movement sequences and the space required.

**Practical . . .**
measuring, marking, cutting, joining, folding

## WHAT HAVE YOU DISCOVERED?

How long does it take to put up the theatre? to put it away?

What problems did you have during the performance?

How could you put these problems

# WHAT A PERFORMANCE!

DESIGN AND MAKE
a mobile puppet theatre.
You must be able to
put it up and pack
it away easily.

THINK ABOUT --- What mechanisms can be used to make it easy to assemble?

THINK ABOUT --- How much space will be needed for the puppets?

# STARTING POINTS ....... An investigation into different methods

of storing and carrying collections of everyday items in the home and at school (sewing boxes, cleaning equipment, tools etc.) . . . Focus on desk items . . . demonstration and discussion of the problems associated with the storage of many small items in one container eg. plastic ice cream container with tangled elastic bands, paper clips etc..... Analysis of the different sizes, shapes and weights of the items to be stored.

## MATERIALS

junk materials eg. cardboard tubes, boxes, plastic containers
stiff card
corrugated card
corruflute
adhesives
(wood)

## THINGS TO THINK ABOUT

Will you need a labelling system?

Will the system be easy to use or is it complicated?

Will it encourage tidiness?

How will you make it stable?

## PREPARATION/EQUIPMENT/OTHER RESOURCES

Display/collection of different storage systems.

Catalogues and magazines advertising storage systems.

Equipment for cutting card and plastic (wood)

## MORE THINGS TO THINK ABOUT

Is the container easy to move from one place to another?

How could you make your design personal?

How will your design be "finished off"?

## SKILLS TO BE DEVELOPED

**Investigational . . .**

Classification of items to be stored.
Analysis of requirements.
Exploration of suitable materials and techniques for construction

**Practical . . .**

marking, measuring, cutting, forming, shaping, assembly.

## WHAT HAVE YOU DISCOVERED?

Which design is the easiest to use? Why?

Which design is the most stable? Why?

Which design is the most portable? Why?

Does your container stay tidy over a period of time?

# KEEP IT TIDY!

Now, Where is it? It was here a few minutes ago........

Paul can never find his pens, pencils, ruler, rubbers, paper clips or anything else as his desk is always in a mess. Is yours?

## DESIGN AND MAKE

a container for pens, pencils, rulers, rubbers, paperclips etc. so that they can be found easily. The container should be designed to stand on a desk but be portable as well.

THINK ABOUT - How many pens, pencils, rulers etc. will have to be stored?

THINK ABOUT - How will the size, shape and weight of the items affect your design?

# STARTING POINTS . . . . . . .

A visit to a D.I.Y. store to observe methods of storing a variety of tools . . . a study of catalogues . . . a school survey of storage methods . . . recording of findings (sketches/lists/oral presentation) . . . Home survey to investigate storage of kitchen utensils etc. . . . . . Emphasise safety aspect of storage as well as efficiency, tidiness etc.

## MATERIALS

(according to 'focus' of task)
junk materials eg. plastic cartons
boxes, bottles and pots)
card
corruflute
wood
dowelling
nails
hooks
sandpaper
varnish/paint

## THINGS TO THINK ABOUT

How much space does one pair of scissors take up?

Where will the scissor holder be kept?

Does this affect your choice?

Test your design for a week.

## PREPARATION/EQUIPMENT/OTHER RESOURCES

Collection of storage systems

Catalogues to show storage systems

Safety knives and rulers

Carpentry tools (according to 'focus' of task)

## MORE THINGS TO THINK ABOUT

How many pairs of scissors will need to be stored?

What about safety? (Scissors are sharp and can be dangerous)

If the system is too complicated, will people bother to use it?

## SKILLS TO BE DEVELOPED

**Investigational . . .**

Observation, identification and analysis of storage methods. Evaluation of suitable designs for scissors.

**Practical . . .**

measuring, marking, cutting, joining and fixing.

## WHAT HAVE YOU DISCOVERED?

Does your design work?

Are all the scissors put away each time?

What do other teachers think about your system?

Could you use your system for other equipment?

# STARTING POINTS ...... A tour of the school cloakroom areas . . .
identification and discussion of tidiness problems . . . pupil survey on items lost
. . interview school caretaker and cleaners . . . a 'brainstorm' session about ways
to encourage tidiness . . . focus on personal identification. . . . (Card labels
could be interpreted in wood once designs are perfected)

## MATERIALS

card (various thicknesses)
corruflute
paper fasteners
adhesive
drawing pins

thin plywood, dowelling and cm$^2$ wood
(according to focus of task)

materials for decoration

## THINGS TO THINK ABOUT

Where will the label be placed?

How much space is available?

What could you use, apart from your
name, to label your peg?

initials?  logos?  symbols?  a photo?

## PREPARATION/EQUIPMENT/OTHER RESOURCES

Arrange interviews and surveys.

Safety knives and rulers
Carpentry equipment
(according to 'focus' of task)

Skill card nos. 1 and 2

## MORE THINGS TO THINK ABOUT

What mechanisms could you use to hide
and reveal your name?

sliding?

rotating?

lifting?

Could you use levers?

## SKILLS TO BE DEVELOPED

**Investigational** . . .

Observation identification and
analysis of cloakroom problems

**Practical** . . .
measuring, marking, cutting, joining
and fixing.

## WHAT HAVE YOU DISCOVERED?

How well does your identification
system work?

Is the cloakroom tidier?

Do people recognise your label?

Do you recognise other people's
labels?

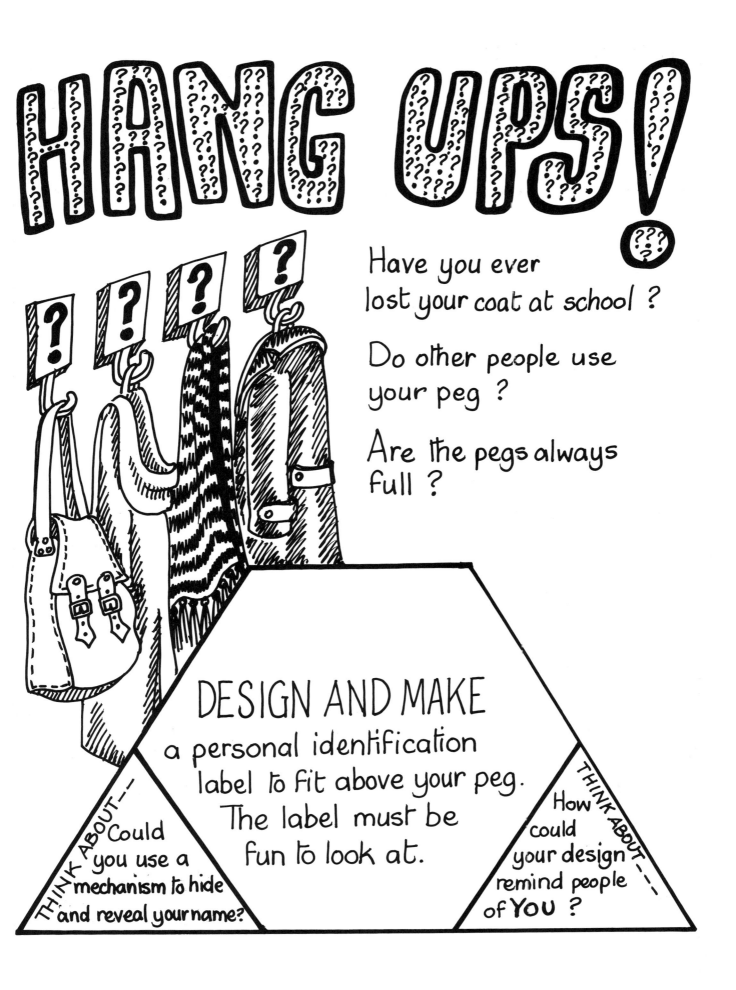

# HANG UPS!

Have you ever lost your coat at school?

Do other people use your peg?

Are the pegs always full?

DESIGN AND MAKE a personal identification label to fit above your peg. The label must be fun to look at.

THINK ABOUT— Could you use a mechanism to hide and reveal your name?

THINK ABOUT— How could your design remind people of YOU?

# STARTING POINTS . . . . . . .

Road safety topic work . . . Green Cross Code . . . Cycling Proficiency . . . road safety practice using playground markings . . interview crossing patrol . . . visiting speaker on road safety . . . focus on poster design . . . analysis of eye-catching features of posters observed in the locality.

## MATERIALS

large sheets of paper or card
collage materials
point
felt-tip pens
lettering stencils

## THINGS TO THINK ABOUT

What do you want someone to learn from your poster?

What colours will you use?

How much writing will be needed? What size?

## PREPARATION/EQUIPMENT/OTHER RESOURCES

Arrange visiting speakers, videos, interviews etc.

Road safety symbols

Collection of advertising material.

## MORE THINGS TO THINK ABOUT

Can your poster be read from a distance?

How could you make it clearer?

What do other people think of your design?

## SKILLS TO BE DEVELOPED

**Investigational . . .**

Identification of dangers
Evaluation of poster designs

**Practical . . .**

drawing, measuring and arranging poster layout to create maximum visual impact.

## WHAT HAVE YOU DISCOVERED?

Which poster is the most eye-catching?  Why?

Have people learned something about road safety from your poster?

# STOP, LOOK AND LISTEN

## STOP

Many adults and children are killed or badly injured on our roads each day. A road safety campaign will draw attention to the dangers of our busy roads.

## DESIGN AND MAKE

a poster that will increase a young child's awareness of road safety in your neighbourhood.

THINK ABOUT - Which colours will be the most eye-catching?

THINK ABOUT - The length of your message. Will people read it?

# STARTING POINTS . . . . . . .

Collection of pictures and photographs of people wearing different types of clothes . . . classification into categories (sports wear, party wear, work wear etc.) . . . encourage discussion of appropriate choices eg. practicality, protection . . . Fabric investigation . . . (hardwearing, washable, waterproof, insulating etc) . . . survey/questionnaire about school uniform . . . (colours, styles etc.)

## MATERIALS

drawing paper
selection of pencils, crayons and pens (highlighter pens)
fabric and wool samples for swatches
buttons and fastenings
adhesive
(sewing equipment)

## THINGS TO THINK ABOUT

Find out which colour would be most popular?

Will the uniform change for summer and winter?

Will the uniform be the same for boys and girls?

What about cost?

## PREPARATION/EQUIPMENT/OTHER RESOURCES

Collection of visual stimulus material.

Fashion magazines and catalogues

Fabrics

Examples of clothing and shoes with different fastenings  (buttons, zips, hooks and eyes, buckles, laces, poppers, velcro etc.)

## MORE THINGS TO THINK ABOUT

Will your designs to easy to wear? easy to put on and take off? (Think about fastenings for young children)

Could you use the school badge in your design?

Try out different colouring techniques to show different fabrics eg. knitted and woven.

## SKILLS TO BE DEVELOPED

**Investigational . . .**

Observation and analysis of different types and styles of clothing.
Planning of survey/questionnaire
Recording and analysis of results.

**Practical . . .**

Drawing and planning of leaflet or poster.

## WHAT HAVE YOU DISCOVERED?

What do pupils, teachers and parents think about your ideas?

Will your designs go out of fashion?

Does your poster or leaflet explain your ideas clearly?

# UNIFORMLY YOU!

Are you always told what to wear?

I am sure that you have a better idea of what you'd like to be seen in.

## DESIGN AND MAKE

a leaflet or poster to show your ideas for a new school uniform for winter and summer.

THINK ABOUT How many items of clothing will you have to design?

THINK ABOUT What do parents, pupils and teachers think about uniforms? Find out _____

# STARTING POINTS . . . . .

A collection of hats . . . analysis of their function (safety, hygiene, identification, protection etc.). . . . . classification according to shape and features (e.g. peak, brim), materials (fabric, paper). . . . Disposable hats can be taken apart and analysed . . Interview with the school cook to discuss the need for head wear in the kitchen. . . . This could be extended to a study of other people who wear hats in their work e.g. police, nurses, postmen and women, factory workers, building site workers etc.

## MATERIALS

paper (various types and thicknesses e.g.sugar paper, newsprint, tissue)
card
adhesive tape
pins
staples
elastic bands
string

## THINGS TO THINK ABOUT

What must the hat be like to do its job properly?

How long will the cook have to wear the hat? (think about comfort)

How can you make sure that the hat will stay in place?

What will happen to the hat when it gets dirty?

## PREPARATION/EQUIPMENT/OTHER RESOURCES

A collection of visual stimulus material ( pictures of a variety of people wearing differnt types of hats)

A collection of hats worn in fast food chains

Disposable hats to take apart and analyse

## MORE THINGS TO THINK ABOUT

Will the hat have any special features? a peak? a logo?

How could you design the hat so that it could be adjusted to fit several different head sizes?

If the cook is willing, test your hat designs in use.

## SKILLS TO BE DEVELOPED

**Investigational. . .**

Research into requirements for hat design. Analysis of hat designs. Hypothesis and testing conversion of a 2-D shape into a 3-D object.

**Practical . . .**

Measuring, marking, cutting, forming, shaping, joining and fixing.

## WHAT HAVE YOU DISCOVERED?

What does the school cook think of your designs?

Was it comfortable to wear?

Did it do its job?

Could you use what you have learnt to design another hat for yourself for a sunny day?

# What's cooking?

DESIGN AND MAKE a hat for the school cook.

THINK ABOUT— What will you have to measure?

THINK ABOUT— Why does the cook need a hat?

# STARTING POINTS . . . . . .

A study of how and where birds feed . . . book research into differnt types of birds and their feeding habits . . . . wildlife videos . . . . a visit to a bird sanctuary . . . writing letters to the RSPB for information . . . . discussion and design of a survey chart to complete during a bird watching session in the school grounds . . . encourage sketches of the birds observed

## MATERIALS

junk materials e.g. plastic cartons, trays, bottles etc.
Wood (various thicknesses)
$cm^2$ wood and dowelling
wire
chicken wire
string
corruflute
adhesive
elastic bands
nails

## THINGS TO THINK ABOUT

What sort of food will you use to feed the birds?

How will you keep the food inside the feeder?

How will the birds be able to reach the food ?  (Think about the different positions birds feed in

## PREPARATION/EQUIPMENT/OTHER RESOURCES

Arrange video recordings

Send for RSPB information pack

Arrange visiting speaker

Cutting tools and other wood working equipment (to be used under supervision)
Sandpaper and varnish

## MORE THINGS TO THINK ABOUT

How could you control the amount of food which is dispensed?

How could your design influence the types of bird attracted to the feeder?

Could you include a method to indicate when the feeder is empty?

## SKILLS TO BE DEVELOPED

**Investigational. . .**

Information and study skills. Observation and recording of bird behaviour.  Interpretation of findings.  Hypothesis and testing of bird feeder design and its position.

**Practical . . .**

Measuring, marking, cutting, forming, joining and fixing.

## WHAT HAVE  YOU DISCOVERED?

Where do different species of birds prefer to feed?

What do different birds prefer to eat?

Which design attracted the most birds?  Why?

Which was the best position for your feeder?

# STARTING POINTS . . . . . . .

A 'dressing up' session using a selection of real hats . . . role-play activity . . . discussion about different hats for different purposes and different characters . . . introduce the character of Mr. Ordinary . . . encourage pencil drawings of ideas for hats for special occasions . . . conduct a 'feasability' talk . . . . . . conduct a 'feasability' talk . . . would Mr. Ordinary be impressed? . . . focus on materials to be used . . .

## MATERIALS

card
adhesive tape
string
junk materials
paper clips
paper fasteners
staples
(batteries, bulbs, wire -depending on 'focus' of task)
materials for decoration

## THINGS TO THINK ABOUT

Could your hat have a theme?

Think about animals, birds, butterflies . . .

How will you turn a flat piece of card into a hat shape?

Will the hat have a brim?

## PREPARATION/EQUIRMENT/OTHER RESOURCES

Collection of hats

tape measures

safety knives and rulers

mirrors

Skill card no. 6

## MORE THINGS TO THINK ABOUT

Could hat have a surprise?
Moving eyes, wings, or a lid?

Could you use light bulbs?  for eyes? a message?

Organise a hat parade.

## SKILLS TO BE DEVELOPED

**Investigational . . .**

existing hat designs.
Hypothesis and testing of hat construction in card

**Practical . . .**

Measuring, marking, cutting, shaping, forming, joining and fixing.

## WHAT HAVE YOU DISCOVERED?

How many different hat shapes has your class produced?

Could you use the techniques you have used on other projects?

# STARTING POINTS ......

A survey of hobbies interests and pastimes enjoyed by members of the class . . . An investigation of symbols and logos (roadsigns, sports club badges, brownie and cub badges etc) . . . . .

## MATERIALS

Card (various thicknesses)
paper
paper fasteners
adhesive tape
glue
safety pins
materials for decoration

## THINGS TO THINK ABOUT

Do badges always have to be round?

What other shapes could be used?

What symbols are usually used to represent your interest?

Can you think of something more unusual?

## PREPARATION/EQUIPMENT/OTHER RESOURCES

Collection of examples of symbols and logos used to represnt ideas eg. travel brochures, Highway Code, Olympic games, hobbies magazines etc.

Shape templates

Safety knives and rulers

Skill card nos. 1, 2 and 6

## MORE THINGS TO THINK ABOUT

Could you make the badge more interesting by including a moving part?
a foot kicking a ball?
waves on the water?
a book which opens?
a dog with a wagging tail?

## SKILLS TO BE DEVELOPED

**Investigational . . .**

Observation and analyisis of symbolic representation of ideas.
Exploration of suitable symbols to represent hobbies

**Practical . . .**
marking, measuring, cutting, joining and fixing.

## WHAT HAVE YOU DISCOVERED?

Does your badge tell others what your interests are?

Can they tell immediately or do they have to guess?

How could you make the badge clearer?

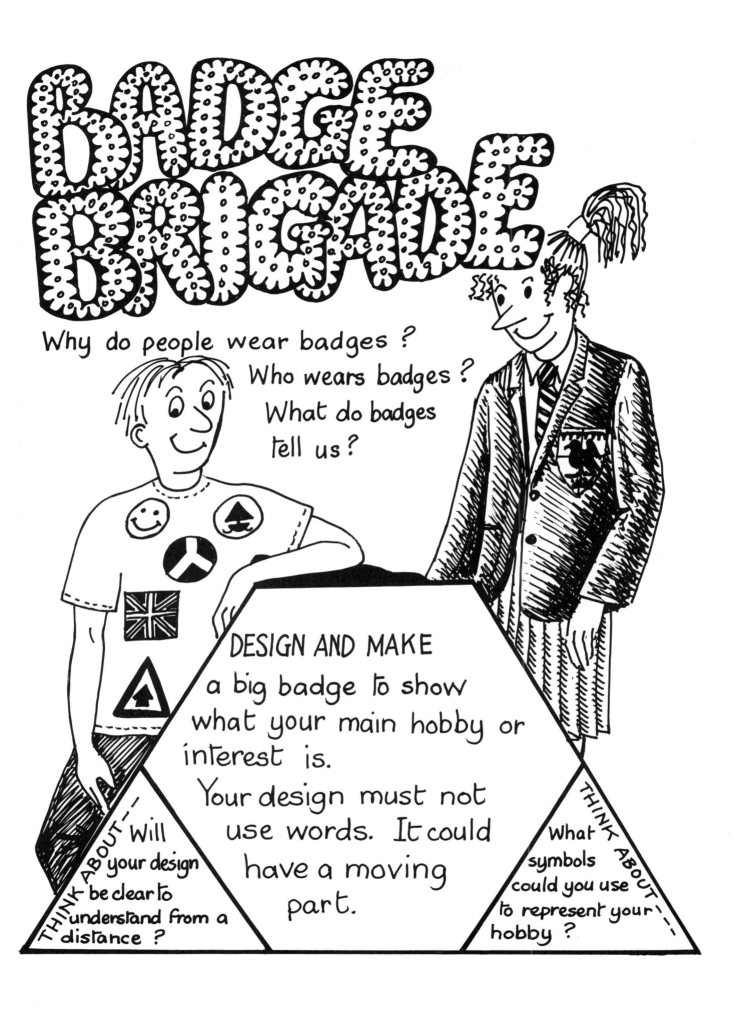

# BADGE BRIGADE

Why do people wear badges?
Who wears badges?
What do badges tell us?

DESIGN AND MAKE
a big badge to show what your main hobby or interest is.
Your design must not use words. It could have a moving part.

THINK ABOUT... Will your design be clear to understand from a distance?

THINK ABOUT... What symbols could you use to represent your hobby?

# STARTING POINTS ........

A collection of money boxes and piggy banks . . . a 'brainstorm' session about novelty collection boxes pupils have seen eg. RNLI RSPCA . . . focus on idea of movement mechanism activated by coins . . . a study of different coins (weight, size etc) . . . Encourage model making to investigate movement mechanisms

## MATERIALS

thick card
corrugated card
paper fasteners
lollipop sticks
cotton reels
dowelling
wire or string
(clay, wood, papier mache, mod-roc -
according to focus of task)

## THINGS TO THINK ABOUT

What should you sort out first?
The movement mechanism or the shape of the box?

Will the coin operate a lever?
a wheel and axle?

## PREPARATION/EQUIPMENT/OTHER RESOURCES

Collection of money boxes

Coins

Commercial construction kits

Safety knives and rulers

Carpentry tools (depending on focus of task)

## MORE THINGS TO THINK ABOUT

Will your system stand up to use over and over again?

Could you include a system for counting the money collected?

Can you include a system to get the money out?

## SKILLS TO BE DEVLEOPED

**Investigational . . .**

Observation and analysis of existing designs.
Hypothesis and testing of ideas for movement mechanism

**Practical . . .**

Marking, measuring, cutting, shaping, forming, joining and fixing.

## WHAT HAVE YOU DISCOVERED?

Does the money box encourage more money to be collected?

Which movement mechanism is the most popular? Why?

# STARTING POINTS . . . . . .

Collection of printed notepaper, letterheads, logos etc .. . discussion on layout, lettering styles etc . . . focus on pupil's own names (shape and pattern of the letters) . . . illuminated manuscripts . . . coats of arms . . . family crests . . .

## MATERIALS

Selection of A4 paper (various colours)
pencils
crayons
pens
rulers
scissors

## THINGS TO THINK ABOUT

How much space would your design take up on the sheet?

Does the paper have to be square or rectangular?

What features could you use as part of your design? your initals?
a hobby?  your home?

## PREPARATION/EQUIPMENT/OTHER RESOURCES

Collection of visual stimulus material (lettering styles, illuminated lettering, monograms, coats of arms, family crests)

Lettering stencils

Envelopes

## MORE THINGS TO THINK ABOUT?

Can you think of a way to reproduce your design?

Could you make an envelope to match your note paper?

(HINT: open out an envelope to find out what shape it is when flat)

## SKILLS TO BE DEVELOPED

**Investigational** . . .

Book research.
Observation and analysis.

**Practical** . . .

drawing and lettering, folding and joining.

## WHAT HAVE YOU DISCOVERED?

Study your designs.  What is the importance of colour?  shape?
balance?

Which design is the most effective?
Why?

Could you use what you have learnt to improve the school notepaper?

# Pen Friends

DESIGN AND MAKE your own personalised writing paper, then use it to write a letter to a friend.

THINK ABOUT— What shape, size and colour will the paper be?

THINK ABOUT— Will friends know the letter is from _you_ without reading it?

# STARTING POINTS ....... A collection of reference material to
study the faces of animals, insects and birds . . . collection of 'eye-wear' (sunglasses, goggles, diners' masks, safety glasses, monocles, visors, magnifying glasses, etc) . . . discussion of famous people who wear spectacles (Dame Edna Everage, Elton John, Sue Pollard) .. . encourage pencil drawings . . .

## MATERIALS

card and paper (various colours and thicknesses)
paper fasteners
staples
adhesive tape
pipe cleaners
straws
junk materials e.g. plastic containers, cardboard tubes etc.
decorative materials e.g. tissue paper, sequins, feathers etc.

## THINGS TO THINK ABOUT

How will the spectacles be kept on? arms?  elastic bands?

Which measurements will you need to take ?
width of nose?  width of head?
nose to ear?  between the eyes?

Does the design have to be symmetrical?

## PREPARATION/EQUIPMENT/OTHER RESOURCES

Collection of visual stimulus material.

Collection of 'eye-wear' examples

Skills card no. 6

## MORE THINGS TO THINK ABOUT

Will your design fit anyone?

How could it be made to fit anyone?

Do you need to think about safety?

Wear your design for a period of time.  Is it comforable?

## SKILLS TO BE DEVELOPED

**Investigational** . . .

Observation and analysis of existing eye-wear designs.
Research for design ideas

**Practical** . . .

drawing, measuring, marking, cutting, joining and fixing.

## WHAT HAVE YOU DISCOVERED?

Which design is the most outrageous?

Which design is the most comfortable to wear?

# Spectacular Spectacles

DESIGN AND MAKE a pair of spectacular glasses for a fancy dress party. Make them as outrageous as you like.

THINK ABOUT— How will the spectacles stay in place?

THINK ABOUT— What shape will the spectacles be?

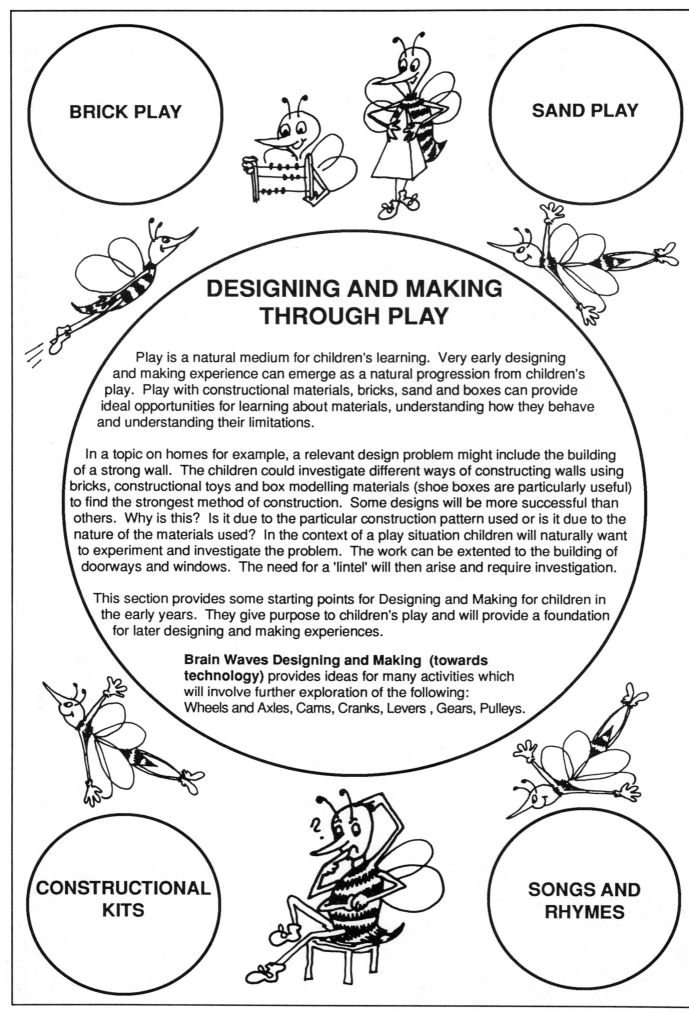

**BRICK PLAY**

**SAND PLAY**

# DESIGNING AND MAKING THROUGH PLAY

Play is a natural medium for children's learning. Very early designing and making experience can emerge as a natural progression from children's play. Play with constructional materials, bricks, sand and boxes can provide ideal opportunities for learning about materials, understanding how they behave and understanding their limitations.

In a topic on homes for example, a relevant design problem might include the building of a strong wall. The children could investigate different ways of constructing walls using bricks, constructional toys and box modelling materials (shoe boxes are particularly useful) to find the strongest method of construction. Some designs will be more successful than others. Why is this? Is it due to the particular construction pattern used or is it due to the nature of the materials used? In the context of a play situation children will naturally want to experiment and investigate the problem. The work can be extented to the building of doorways and windows. The need for a 'lintel' will then arise and require investigation.

This section provides some starting points for Designing and Making for children in the early years. They give purpose to children's play and will provide a foundation for later designing and making experiences.

**Brain Waves Designing and Making (towards technology)** provides ideas for many activities which will involve further exploration of the following:
Wheels and Axles, Cams, Cranks, Levers , Gears, Pulleys.

**CONSTRUCTIONAL KITS**

**SONGS AND RHYMES**

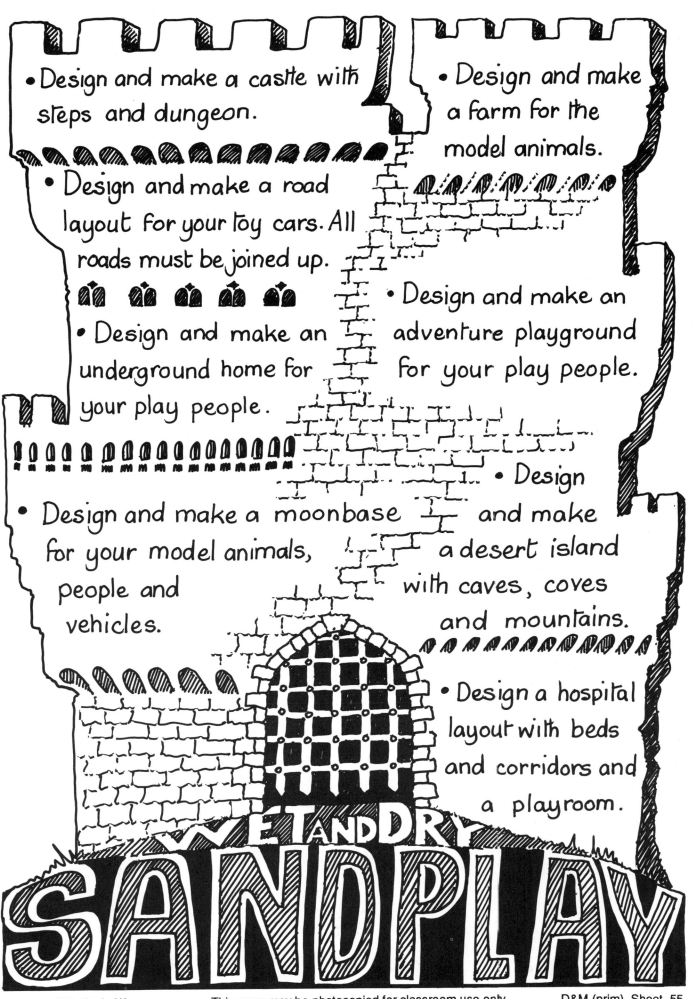

- Design and make a castle with steps and dungeon.

- Design and make a farm for the model animals.

- Design and make a road layout for your toy cars. All roads must be joined up.

- Design and make an underground home for your play people.

- Design and make an adventure playground for your play people.

- Design and make a moonbase for your model animals, people and vehicles.

- Design and make a desert island with caves, coves and mountains.

- Design a hospital layout with beds and corridors and a playroom.

# WET AND DRY SANDPLAY

Design and make a castle with a bridge, ramparts and a tower.

Design and make a garage with petrol pumps, a car wash and a workshop with an inspection pit.

Design and make a free standing structure as tall as yourself.

Design and make a hide so that you cannot be seen but you can see out !

Design and make a road layout including a busy junction and a fly-over bridge.

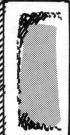

Design and make a building with two floors and a staircase connecting them.

**BRICK PLAY**

Design and make the widest bridge you can.

**LARGE**

Design and make a wall. Find the strongest pattern of bricks.

Design and make a moon base, including a control room, a living room and sleeping quarters.

**SMALL SMALL SMALL SMALL SMALL**

Design and make a farmyard for visitors with a circular route.

Design and make a staircase with as many steps as you can.

Design and build a cafe big enough for four people.

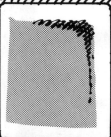

Design and make a ramp for the start of a car race. Can you include a structure that will stop the cars slowly ?

Design and make a cosy place to talk and read with friends.

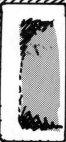

Design and make a fire engine.

Design and make a house for your Teddy Bear or doll.

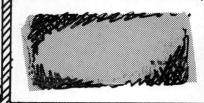

# CONSTRUCTIONAL PLAY

Design and make a double-decker bus.

Design and make a tower with triangular shapes in its construction.

Design and make a jib crane with a hook and pulley strong enough to pick up a 500g weight.

Design and make the tallest look out tower you can but stable enough to carry a 200g. weight.

Design and make a breakdown vehicle that will pull another model car.

Design and make the widest bridge you can. It must be self-supporting. Try making a bridge which opens and closes.

Design and make a four-engined aeroplane with propellers and big enough to carry six model people.

Design and make a model adventure playground. Include climbing, swinging, balancing and sliding activities.

Design and make some four wheeled vehicles from different constructional materials. Using a ramp find out how far and easy the vehicles run across the floor. Change the designs to improve the performance.

Design a hospital layout. Include a ward with beds and private rooms, a place for outpatients, a coffee bar and a playroom for children.

Design and make a crane or digger that will pick up fine material (eg. sand, split peas, plastic packaging pieces).

Design and make a vehicle with six wheels and with two wheels that will lift up from the ground.

**Ding Dong Dell**
Design and make a device for lifting poor pussy from the well.

**If you go down in the woods today.**
Design and make a rain cover for the Teddy Bear's picnic. Your materials are sellotape, plastic bags and newspaper.

**In a dark dark wood**
Design and make a light with a switch for the dark, dark room.

**Jack and Jill**
Design and make a vehicle or device for transporting two small buckets of water down the hill.

**Humpty Dumpty**
Design and make a lift or crane to help Humpty back on the wall.

**Mary, Mary.**
Redesign Mary's garden. Try a plan view.

**Grand Old Duke of York.**
Design and make a vehicle or device for carrying twenty model soldiers to the top of the hill.

# Designing and Making from Songs & Rhymes

**Old Macdonald**
Design and make a farmyard for Old Macdonald's animals.

**Sing a song of sixpence**
Design and make a model pie with a pop-up blackbird.

**Three Blind Mice**
Design and make a model of a trapping device.

**We're going on a lion hunt**
Design and make a bridge to cross the river. Try making some lights for the dark cave.

**The wheels on the bus go round and round**
Design and make a model of a double decker bus with moving wheels.

**Dingle Dangle Scarecrow**
Design the scarecrow a new set of clothes for the outdoors.

**When Goldilocks went to the house with three bears**
Design and make a model of a chair or bed. Use a doll for Goldilocks to test your model.

# HIDE AND REVEAL (by sliding)

**PROBLEM TO SOLVE:**
How will you make sure that there is **room** to "hide" the object or message?

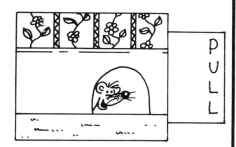

---

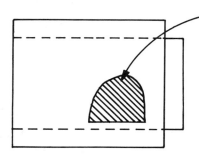

cut window out of card

Place a card "slider" behind window.

Mark the window in pencil before the "slider" is pulled (1) and after the "slider" is pulled (2).

(They may overlap)

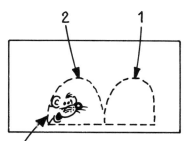

draw picture in window 2
Rub out pencil markings

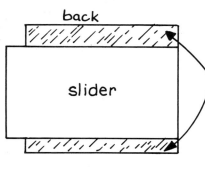

Place the slider face down on the back of the card.
Glue the back of the card not covered by the slider.

Cover the back with a new piece of card.

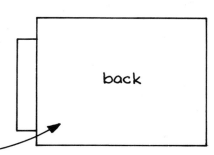

OR

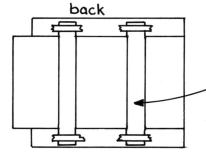

Place the slider face down on the back of the card.
Make "guides" using strips of card and adhesive tape.

**PROBLEM TO SOLVE:**
How could you stop the slider being pulled right out?

This page may be photocopied for classroom use only

# HIDE AND REVEAL (by rotation)

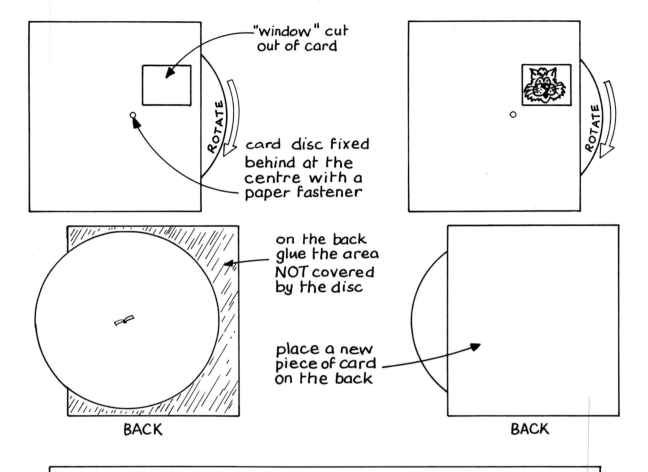

"window" cut out of card

ROTATE

card disc fixed behind at the centre with a paper fastener

ROTATE

on the back glue the area NOT covered by the disc

place a new piece of card on the back

BACK

BACK

---

**PROBLEM TO SOLVE :** How can you work out where to draw the object on the card disc ?

---

IDEAS :

we are :  OPEN

Super Shop

rotate the fins of the fish to change the message

OPEN

OR clown juggling birds flying

---

This page may be photocopied for classroom use only

# MAKING A BOOK

Books can be made from folded sheets of paper

Planning a 16 page book :

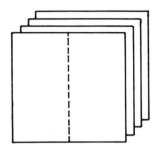

Put four sheets of paper in a pile.

Fold the pile in half.

Number all the pages from 1 to 16.

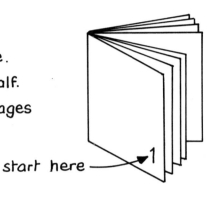

start here ⟶ 1

Open out and separate the sheets

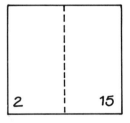
2 | 15

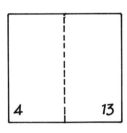
4 | 13

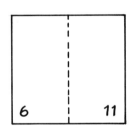
6 | 11

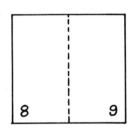
8 | 9

What are the page numbers on the back of each sheet?

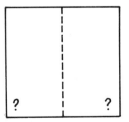
? | ?

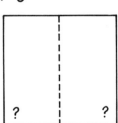
? | ?

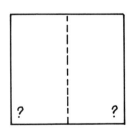
? | ?

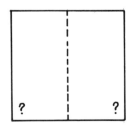
? | ?

PROBLEM TO SOLVE :
How will the book be held together?

books can be "stitched" or wire stapled

# SPINNERS

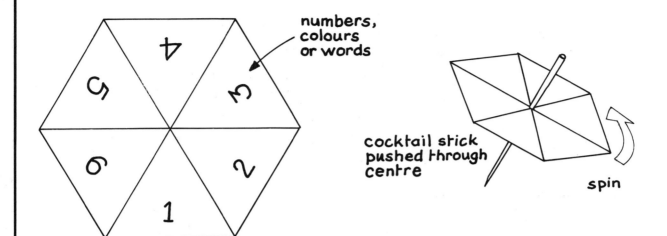

numbers, colours or words

cocktail stick pushed through centre

spin

## Use the hexagons below to make your spinner

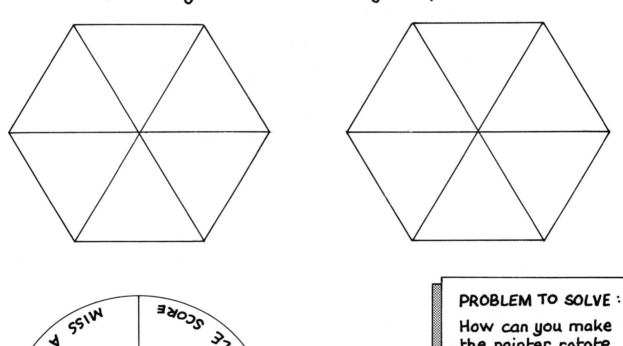

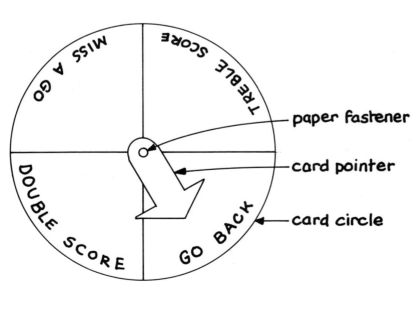

paper fastener

card pointer

card circle

TREBLE SCORE

MISS A GO

DOUBLE SCORE

GO BACK

**PROBLEM TO SOLVE:**

How can you make the pointer rotate freely?

Try using other materials instead of a paper fastener.

---

This page may be photocopied for classroom use only

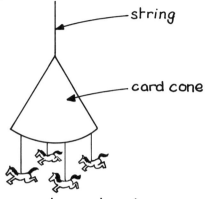

string

card cone

paper shapes hanging on thread

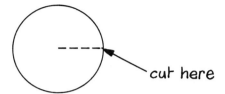

cut here

roll and shape to form a cone and stick with tape or glue

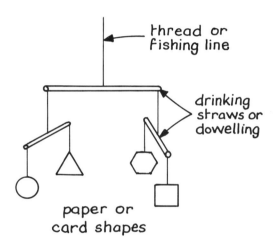

thread or fishing line

drinking straws or dowelling

paper or card shapes

**PROBLEM TO SOLVE:** How can you balance the mobile?

**HINT:** Try plasticine weights.

**PROBLEM TO SOLVE:** How can the mobile make a noise? Experiment with different materials.

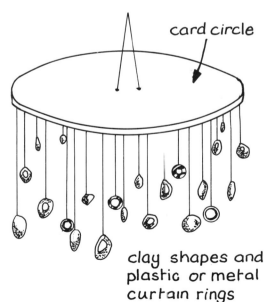

card circle

clay shapes and plastic or metal curtain rings

# HINGES AND PIVOTS

skill card 6

## Hinges to open and close

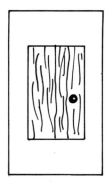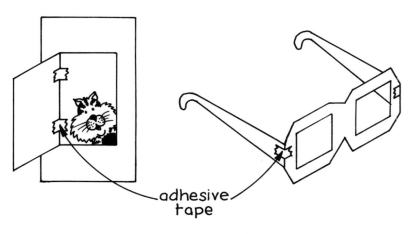

adhesive tape

## Hinges to change a message

↑
pull string to change expression

draw a sad face on a card circle

draw a happy smile on a half circle.

Stick onto sad face with tape

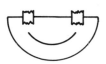

PROBLEM TO SOLVE : What do you draw on the other side?

## Pivots for movement

toilet roll tube or drinking straw

paper fastener pivots

string

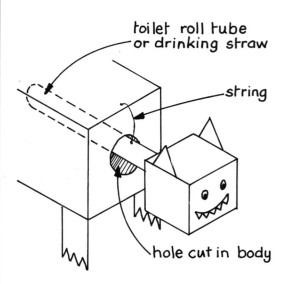

hole cut in body

PROBLEM TO SOLVE : How can you make the head balance?

HINT: Use a plasticine weight

© S.E.P. Brain Waves · This page may be photocopied for classroom use only · Sheet 64